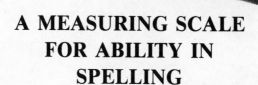

A MEASURING SCALE
FOR ABILITY IN
SPELLING

A MEASURING SCALE FOR ABILITY IN SPELLING

LEONARD P. AYRES

Originally published by
Russell Sage Foundation

This edition published by

MOTT
MEDIA

This edition copyright © 1986 by Mott Media, Inc.
1000 East Huron Street, Milford, Michigan 48042

ISBN 0-88062-039-0
Printed in the United States of America

PRESENT PUBLISHER'S FOREWORD

Do children today spell as well as school children of 1915? Now with this republication of Ayres' scale it will be possible to find out.

Most research in our time makes comparisons only within recent decades. Thus it is difficult to show whether education has improved or deteriorated as compared to the early part of this century. But now with this unique tool, you can test your pupils' spelling ability and make that comparison. Using the scale is simple once you see how to read the heading of the scale and see how the word lists are arranged. For ease of use, we have added an appendix in which the scale is repeated in a chart form. Almost immediately you can give your children a ten- or twenty-word test and see how they measure against school children of 1915.

I invite you to send me the results of testing that you do with this scale. Along with the scores, please send information about the children's grade levels and about the spelling system they have been trained with. I hope to share such information in future publications. Besides testing, this scale may also be used for teaching. Since the 1000 words in the lists were selected as the most commonly used words, they comprise a high utility list. Students who can spell these words are able to spell from memory a high percentage of words in their daily writing. Therefore, many teachers have been urging us to publish Ayres' scale.

For the numerous parents and teachers who are concerned about the state of education, particularly the state of basic literacy skills, we proudly present this reissue of a true American educational classic.

I express my gratitude to Geraldine E. Rodgers, a remarkable first grade teacher whose pupils are excellent spellers. Rodgers has contributed valuable research on Leonard P. Ayres, his times, and his spelling scale.

George M. Mott, President
Mott Media Inc.

PREFACE

The great phonics debate has raged for centuries in spelling as it has in reading. In America, it dates almost as far back as Noah Webster's first spelling book in 1783. Webster's system was based on phonics, and for about a century, imitators and others who followed Webster continued to use phonics methods. In fact, phonics and spelling were THE route to reading in those days. Children first learned sounds and then blended them into syllables. Once children could read and spell syllables, it was assumed they were ready to practice them on connected reading—in portions of the Bible, for instance. It apparently seldom occurred to anyone to give children *word* lists to read, because reading was for those people what spelling was: the reading and spelling of *syllables*.

In about the middle of the 1800s, when government schools were replacing private schools, the sight word method of reading came into wide use. Teachers learned the new ways at normal schools and summer institutes, and spelling based on sound as an *introduction* to reading largely disappeared. But the debate did not disappear. Horace Mann, Edward Thorndike, John Dewey, and other great names in education were on the "word" side of the debate. Rebecca Pollard and other lesser known names were on the "sound" side of the debate. Nevertheless, by the turn of the century the pendulum had swung back to phonics and children were spelling well again.

At this time there appeared on the scene a man uniquely qualified to turn the eyes of research on the spelling problem: Leonard Ayres (1879-1946) successful teacher, school administrator, statistician, and researcher. In 1908, he became director of the Department of Education and Statistics of the Russell Sage Foundation and conducted studies in 250 cities. During this time he directed the research which is described in this book. In World War I, he was statistical officer for several government boards and commissions. After the war he returned to the Russell Sage Foundation for a period, and still later he organized his own statistical service.

In 1915 when this work was originally published, the September issue of the *Elementary School Journal* had this to say about it:

> . . . it may be said in a word that Dr. Ayers has ferreted out the thousand words in most common use in the every-day world and has by numerous tests arranged these in the order of increasing difficulty, marking off the points at which successive grades are found to miss different percentages of each list. The book will be the basis of spelling teaching in every school system. The method of setting up a scale is also most significant. There is no statistical elaboration of opinion at the bottom of this classification, but a systematic series of experiments with school children. The book is one which will be welcomed by practical teachers and by students of scientific methods.

Following Ayres, the new-style basal readers once again popularized the word method. Thus the scale is historically significant for us, providing scores for children of 1915, who were still taught by the phonics method. The proponents of the sight word approach looked to Ayres' scale for both testing and teaching. And now, proponents of phonics can use the same scale to see what has happened with the sight word approach of our century. Has it improved spelling? DO OUR CHILDREN SPELL AS WELL AS THOSE AYRES TESTED? The document in this little book holds the answers to such questions.

This once-famous Ayres' spelling scale had virtually disappeared when I began my search for a copy. Even its listing in education bibliographies disappeared by 1938. At the Library of Congress someone handed me what looked like Ayres' spelling scale, but inside was Ayres' handwriting scale, instead. I could see from remnants of stitching in the binding that the original contents had been removed. Columbia University still has a copy, but they have shortened the title to *Ayres Spelling Ability*, so some searchers may miss it. And the New York library rare book collection has it filed under "Russell Sage Foundation," rather than under "Ayres" or "spelling." So that copy was pretty well lost, too.

No doubt, a few other copies exist in rare book rooms around the country, but nothing, of course, has been generally available and usable for the public. So this edition by Mott Media is a welcome event.

1986   *Geraldine E. Rodgers*
                                    Lyndhurst, New Jersey

A MEASURING SCALE FOR ABILITY IN SPELLING

During 1914 and the earlier months of 1915 the Division of Education of the Russell Sage Foundation has been conducting a study of spelling among school children with the object of developing a scale for measuring attainment in the spelling of common words. The object of this report is to describe the investigation and to present the scale which it has produced.

As a first step, it was decided to select a large number of the commonest words and to have them spelled by many school children in order to locate standards of spelling attainment in the several grades. In undertaking this work, it seemed worth while to have the children spell not merely common words, but the commonest words, in order to have the entire study based on what may be termed a foundation spelling vocabulary.

A Foundation Vocabulary

One thousand words were finally selected as constituting such a foundation vocabulary. They were chosen by combining the results of the four most extensive studies that have attempted to identify the words most commonly used in different sorts of English writing.

The first of these studies was published by the Rev. J. Knowles in London, England, in 1904 in a pamphlet entitled, "The London Point System of Reading for the Blind." The author says of it, "Taking passages from the English Bible and from various authors, containing 100,000 words, a list was made of the 353 words which occurred most frequently, and the number of times each occurred was noted."

The second of the studies was made by R. C. Eldridge of Niagara Falls and the results were published in 1911 in a pamphlet entitled, "Six Thousand Common English Words." Mr. Eldridge made an analysis of the vocabularies of 250 different articles taken from four issues of four Sunday newspapers published in Buffalo. He found that they contained a total vocabulary of 6,002 different words, which with their repetitions made an aggregate of 43,989 running words. He reported the number of times that each word appeared.

The third study was conducted by the present writer in 1913 and the results were published by the Division of Education of the Russell Sage Foundation in a monograph entitled, "The Spelling Vocabularies of Personal and Business Letters." The study consisted of the tabulation of 23,629 words from 2,000 short letters written by 2,000 people. The total vocabulary used was found to consist of 2,001 different words and the number of appearances of each was reported.

The last of these four studies was carried through by W. A. Cook and M. V. O'Shea and the results presented in 1914 in a book entitled, "The Child and His Spelling," published by the Bobbs-Merrill Company. This study consisted of the tabulation of some 200,000 words taken from the family correspondence of 13 adults. The total vocabulary was found to consist of 5,200 different words and the number of times each occurred was reported.

Frequent Use of a Few Words

There is one salient characteristic common to all of these studies. This is the cumulative evidence that a few words do most of our work when we write. In every one of the studies it was found that about nine words recur so frequently that they constitute in the aggregate one-fourth of the whole number of words written, while about 50 words constitute with their repetitions one-half of all the words we write. With the exception of *very*, these words are all monosyllables.

It seems reasonable to argue from such evidence that we should do well to find out from such studies as these which words those are that constitute the foundation vocabulary used in ordinary English writing and teach them in our schools so thoroughly that the children by everyday use would permanently master them. It seems equally clear that such a list of words forms a better basis for determining standards of spelling attainment than would one made of less commonly used words. For these reasons it was determined to combine the results of the several studies so as to secure the most reliable available list as a foundation for the work.

At first the purpose was to identify the 2,000 most commonly used words, but this project was abandoned because it was soon found to be impossible of realization. It is easily possible to identify the 10 commonest words in written English. These are probably *the*, *and*, *of*, *to*, *I*, *a*, *in*, *that*, *you*, *for*. With their repetitions they constitute more than one-fourth of all the words we write. Save for the personal pronouns, they are essential in writing about any subject, whatever its nature, from Aaron through zythum. It is likewise possible to identify the 50 commonest words, for, like the first 10, they are true construction words and necessary, no matter what the nature of the subject under consideration. With progressively decreasing reliability the list may be extended to include the 500 commonest words and possibly the 1,000 commonest, but not the 2,000 commonest, for long before this point is reached the identity of the frequently used words varies according to the subject under consideration. For this reason it was decided to limit the foundation vocabulary to 1,000 words.

The Thousand Commonest Words

The list of 1,000 words finally selected was determined upon by finding the frequency with which each word appeared in the tabulations of each study, weighting that frequency according to the size of the base of which it was a part, adding the four frequencies thus obtained, and finding their average. The resulting figure shows how many times the word was repeated in each 100,000 words of written English. The aggregate amount of written material analyzed in securing these results was approximately 368,000 words, written by some 2,500 different persons. More than two-thirds of the material consisted of personal and business letters.

The tabulation of these frequencies furnished a list of several thousand words which were arranged in the descending order of the frequencies with which they occurred. From the list the

1,000 commonest words were selected and have been used as the basis for the present study. These words, together with the figures showing the frequency of appearance of each, per 100,000 running words, are given in List A beginning on page 5. The figures inserted after each 50 words show the cumulative frequencies from the beginning. Thus the first of these figures shows that the 50 commonest words are repeated so frequently that with their repetitions they constitute nearly half of all the words we write. The first 300 words make up more than three-fourths of all writing of this kind and the 1,000 words with their repetitions constitute more than nine-tenths of this sort of written material.

In making up this list, there has been no attempt to reduce all the words to a dictionary basis. Instead the attempt has been to include all the forms of the words which present different spelling difficulties. Thus the various forms of the verb "be" are included as separate words because they present separate spelling difficulties. In the same way "man" and "men," "woman" and "women," are included for the same reason. On the other hand, plurals and verb forms presenting no characteristic spelling difficulties beyond those inherent in the singular or infinitive have not been included. This procedure has necessitated making many arbitrary decisions, but in each case the controlling purpose has been to make each decision on the basis of spelling difficulty.

While the frequencies appearing in List A have been derived as described, it should be explained that not all of the commonest words of the Cook-O'Shea list appear in this new list. This is because their publication did not appear until the present work was well under way and most of the spelling tests had been concluded. However, careful efforts have been made to include all words appearing so frequently that the evidence seemed to warrant their inclusion. While the present list of commonest words can be improved upon, still it is believed to be more reliable as a foundation spelling vocabulary than any one of the previous lists.

LIST A. The thousand commonest words arranged in the descending order of their frequency. The figures indicate the number of occurrences per each hundred thousand running words. The figures inserted after each fifty words are cumulative frequencies from the beginning.

the	6,393	had	397	letter	188
and	3,438	has	391	make	185
of	3,422	very	383	write	182
to	3,217	been	370	thing	181
I	2,387	were	368	think	180
a	1,911	would	362	should	178
in	1,904	she	359	truly	178
that	1,422	or	348	now	177
you	1,306	there	341	its	175
for	1,241	her	311	two	173
it	1,197	an	298	take	172
was	991			thank	170
is	931		49,615	do	169
will	873	when	288	after	168
as	854	time	279	than	167
have	846	go	277	sir	163
not	831	some	273	last	161
with	822	any	257	house	160
be	816	can	250	just	160
your	793	what	244	over	160
at	698	send	242	then	159
we	695	out	238	work	158
on	667	them	238	day	157
he	619	him	233	here	157
by	611	more	232		59,591
but	572	about	220		
my	557	no	220	said	153
this	551	please	211	only	151
his	543	week	211	well	151
which	540	night	206	am	147
dear	523	their	205	these	146
from	488	other	203	tell	145
are	468	up	201	even	144
all	448	our	200	made	144
me	444	good	198	know	143
so	432	say	198	year	143
one	428	could	193	before	138
if	408	who	192	long	137
they	400	may	189	sincerely	135

shall	133	ever	97	four	75
sent	131	girl	97		70,122
us	131	also	96		
give	130	where	96	kind	75
Mr.	129	while	96	oblige	75
like	128	did	95	nothing	74
enclose	126	little	95	off	74
next	125	look	94	believe	73
want	125	respectfully	94	boy	73
hope	122	afternoon	93	city	73
love	121	Miss	93	found	72
men	121	those	93	pay	72
old	118	too	93	tomorrow	71
every	117	man	92	doctor	70
find	117	own	92	five	70
most	117	receive	91	o'clock	70
such	117	soon	91	read	70
today	117	once	89	back	69
must	116	street	88	enough	69
way	116	ask	87	fine	69
first	115	down	87	order	69
new	113	yet	87	bed	68
seem	113	see	86	cold	68
morning	112	since	86	live	68
school	112	cannot	85	mail	68
great	111	help	85	few	67
wish	110	away	83	hear	66
home	109	course	83	child	65
feel	106	through	83	mother	65
glad	106	call	82	return	65
never	106	meet	82	same	65
three	106	people	80	almost	64
much	105	another	79	because	64
how	103	number	78	big	64
until	103	place	78	Monday	64
many	102	Sunday	78	month	64
put	102	use	78	start	64
	65,759	church	77	always	63
		nice	77	both	63
get	101	sure	77	cordially	63
into	99	anything	76	expect	63
let	98	hour	76	mean	63
yesterday	98	children	75	quite	63
come	97	don't	75	Saturday	63

again	62	answer	50	possible	43
Friday	62	half	50	September	43
something	62	keep	50	sick	43
talk	62	life	50	visit	43
though	62	ago	49	went	43
office	61	business	49	act	42
Tuesday	61	does	49	begin	42
best	60	each	49	desire	42
came	60	eight	49	eat	42
	73,452	knew	49	guess	42
		picture	49	hard	42
says	60	show	49	line	42
car	59	build	48	mind	42
ground	59	care	48	October	42
room	59	eye	48	poor	42
thought	59	gentleman	48	remember	42
under	59	head	48	Wednesday	42
board	58			women	42
far	58		76,111	wonder	42
nine	58			conference	41
without	58	left	48	died	41
arrest	57	whether	48	glass	41
trip	57	interest	47	held	41
cent	56	January	47	less	41
right	56	present	47	understand	41
side	56	teacher	47		78,302
Thursday	56	tire	47		
friend	55	upon	47	along	40
bad	54	young	47	August	40
late	54	done	46	evening	40
money	54	high	46	father	40
need	54	sorry	46	forenoon	40
still	54	train	46	large	40
book	53	whom	46	meant	40
hand	53	broke	45	seven	40
mile	53	during	45	address	39
paper	53	feet	45	charge	39
party	53	itself	45	family	39
word	53	several	45	finish	39
madam	52	brought	44	hot	39
six	52	everything	44	known	39
ten	52	run	44	least	39
why	52	took	44	plan	39
perhaps	51	better	43	saw	39
		lost	43		

seen	39	small	34	fact	30
whole	39	summer	34	herself	30
whose	39	together	34	immediate	30
action	38	against	33	marriage	30
change	38	clean	33	May	30
court	38	decide	33	provision	30
follow	38	issue	33	reason	30
matter	38	Mrs.	33	slide	30
cost	37	near	33	story	30
February	37	prompt	33	unfortunate	30
lady	37	question	33	arrange	29
part	37	ring	33	awful	29
reply	37	sit	33	complete	29
spend	37	stamp	33	fire	29
attend	36	turn	33	forget	29
case	36	winter	33	gave	29
fall	36	busy	32	kill	29
however	36	folks	32	mere	29
July	36	happy	32	nearly	29
report	36	lake	32	neither	29
speak	36	maybe	32	noon	29
vote	36	obtain	32	past	29
wife	36	pass	32	service	29
bring	35	ran	32	unless	29
company	35	study	32	aunt	28
cut	35	become	31	ball	28
member	35	December	31	character	28
November	35	dress	31	full	28
open	35	early	31	further	28
reach	35	either	31	learn	28
regard	35	end	31	often	28
women	35	except	31	principle	28
according	34	farther	31	ride	28
	80,175	heard	31	second	28
		March	31	sister	28
between	34	person	31	size	28
bill	34	rather	31	state	28
certain	34	water	31	thus	28
copy	34	written	31	yes	28
deal	34	April	30	afraid	27
director	34	Christmas	30	annual	27
might	34		81,794	automobile	27
move	34			coming	27
rain	34	country	30	date	27

heart	27	west	25	stop	23
law	27	world	25	trust	23
name	27	accept	24	try	23
running	27	alone	24	walk	23
separate	27	arrive	24	warm	23
	83,220	began	24	weather	23
		carry	24	condition	22
sold	27	distribute	24	different	22
told	27	earliest	24	else	22
although	26	effort	24	especially	22
among	26	hat	24	game	22
association	26	justice	24	grant	22
close	26	lose	24	indeed	22
club	26		84,479	liberty	22
dollar	26			necessary	22
evidence	26	lot	24	object	22
form	26	material	24	paid	22
himself	26	nor	24	plant	22
intend	26	sometimes	24	popular	22
June	26	struck	24	post	22
list	26	unable	24	pretty	22
public	26	various	24		85,621
station	26	anyway	23		
table	26	band	23	prison	22
true	26	boat	23	road	22
already	25	dark	23	section	22
appreciate	25	difference	23	subject	22
body	25	door	23	success	22
clear	25	enter	23	supply	22
cover	25	face	23	system	22
driven	25	husband	23	tax	22
fair	25	importance	23	allow	21
getting	25	lead	23	amount	21
got	25	light	23	appoint	21
instead	25	offer	23	expense	21
pleasant	25	pleasure	23	felt	21
price	25	prepare	23	fifth	21
relative	25	refer	23	fill	21
rule	25	represent	23	front	21
son	25	rest	23	information	21
song	25	river	23	miss	21
sudden	25	scene	23	none	21
throw	25	special	23	press	21
war	25	stand	23	red	21

salary	21	across	19	general	18
secure	21	around	19	objection	18
set	21	card	19	perfect	18
tenth	21	cause	19	period	18
ticket	21	death	19	rapid	18
usual	21	divide	19	region	18
wait	21	doubt	19	remain	18
worth	21	drown	19	repair	18
beside	20	easy	19	sail	18
bought	20	escape	19	search	18
built	20	free	19	short	18
buy	20	gone	19	stood	18
carried	20	happen	19	suppose	18
destroy	20	hurt	19	view	18
direction	20	led	19	white	18
fell	20	low	19	able	17
fourth	20	mention	19	above	17
grand	20	promise	19	assure	17
hold	20	result	19	auto	17
inform	20	select	19	baby	17
lay	20	serve	19	catch	17
leave	20	soap	19	duty	17
length	20	suggest	19	education	17
loss	20	teach	19	extra	17
mine	20	terrible	19	fail	17
ought	20	therefore	19	foot	17
outside	20	uncle	19	forward	17
pair	20	absence	18	goes	17
probably	20	article	18	government	17
	86,658	became	18	impossible	17
		behind	18	include	17
ready	20	brother	18	income	17
real	20	dead	18	increase	17
request	20	delay	18	inside	17
spring	20	drill	18	investigate	17
stay	20	effect	18	judgment	17
stole	20	employ	18	navy	17
themselves	20		87,610	omit	17
third	20			opinion	17
top	20	entire	18	police	17
toward	20	entrance	18	position	17
watch	20	extreme	18	power	17
wrote	20	fix	18	prefer	17
account	19	forty	18	proper	17

push	17	spent	16	begun	14
	88,480	stopped	16	belong	14
		vacation	16	camp	14
raise	17	weigh	16	cast	14
really	17	wind	16	circular	14
round	17	wonderful	16	class	14
shut	17	add	15	clothing	14
tonight	17	affair	15	collect	14
total	17	attempt	15	colonies	14
trouble	17		89,284	combination	14
aboard	16			comfort	14
air	16			complaint	14
appear	16	black	15	consideration	14
beautiful	16	claim	15	disappoint	14
burn	16	common	15	distinguish	14
capture	16	convenient	15	due	14
career	16	convention	15	feature	14
check	16	daughter	15	field	14
contain	16	declare	15		90,011
deep	16	estate	15		
direct	16	event	15	firm	14
dozen	16	factory	15	human	14
east	16	favor	15	manner	14
elect	16	God	15	neighbor	14
election	16	illustrate	15	progress	14
engage	16	injure	15	recent	14
express	16	lesson	15	sea	14
final	16	minute	15	session	14
finally	16	news	15	statement	14
gold	16	political	15	suit	14
horse	16	prove	15	theater	14
motion	16	rate	15	visitor	14
north	16	soft	15	agreement	13
occupy	16	suffer	15	alike	13
preliminary	16	surprise	15	allege	13
principal	16	tree	15	application	13
proceed	16	wear	15	argument	13
provide	16	within	15	arrangement	13
refuse	16	yard	15	beg	13
relief	16	age	14	chief	13
retire	16	athletic	14	cities	13
shed	16	attention	14	clerk	13
sight	16	avenue	14	command	13
south	16	bear	14	committee	13

concern	13	restrain	13	land	12
consider	13	royal	13	ledge	12
contract	13	secretary	13	local	12
crowd	13	spell	13	machine	12
dash	13	stone	13	majority	12
debate	13	summon	13	mayor	12
decision	13	testimony	13	measure	12
degree	13	track	13	mountain	12
department	13	travel	13	national	12
diamond	13	victim	13	official	12
difficulty	13	accident	12	organize	12
discussion	13	addition	12	page	12
district	13	adopt	12	particular	12
elaborate	13	army	12	point	12
emergency	13	assist	12	population	12
empire	13	associate	12	pound	12
engine	13	await	12	practical	12
enjoy	13	beginning	12	president	12
entertain	13	block	12	print	12
entitle	13	blow	12	private	12
estimate	13	blue	12	property	12
experience	13	born	12	publication	12
fight	13	box	12	publish	12
figure	13	bridge	12	purpose	12
file	13	celebration	12	race	12
flight	13	center	12	railroad	12
	90,673	century	12	recommend	12
		chain	12	recover	12
flower	13	circumstance	12	reference	12
foreign	13	citizen	12	senate	12
guest	13	connection	12	serious	12
history	13	convict	12	ship	12
important	13	develop	12	steamer	12
imprison	13	examination	12	support	12
improvement	13		91,299	term	12
jail	13			town	12
newspaper	13	famous	12	treasure	12
organization	13	fortune	12	vessel	12
personal	13	height	12	volume	12
piece	13	honor	12	wire	12
play	13	ice	12	witness	12
primary	13	inspect	12	wreck	12
receipt	13	invitation	12		91,899
responsible	13	judge	12		

Cooperation of City Superintendents

When the 1,000 words had been selected, letters were written to city superintendents of schools throughout the country asking if they would cooperate in the work by having lists of 20 words each given as spelling tests in all the grades of their school systems from the second through the eight. Almost without exception they generously agreed to undertake this part of the work, and satisfactory returns were finally secured from the following 84 cities:

Albany, N.Y.
Asbury Park, N.J.
Atlanta, Ga.
Auburn, N.Y.
Augusta, Ga.
Bangor, Me.
Bay City, Mich.
Bayonne, N.J.
Boise, Idaho
Bridgeport, Ct.
Brockton, Mass.
Burlington, Vt.
Cedar Rapids, Iowa
Chicopee, Mass.
Colorado Springs, Colo.
Columbus, Ohio
Covington, Ky.
Cripple Creek, Colo.
Cumberland, Md.
Danville, Ill.
Denver, Colo.
Des Moines, Iowa
Detroit, Mich.
Dubuque, Iowa
Duluth, Minn.
East Orange, N.J.
Elizabeth, N.J.
Evanston, Ill.
Evansville, Ind.
Fall River, Mass.
Fitchburg, Mass.
Fort Wayne, Ind.
Galesburg, Ill.
Grand Rapids, Mich.

Greenwich, Ct.
Harrisburg, Pa.
Haverhill, Mass.
Indianapolis, Ind.
Jackson, Mich.
Jersey City, N.J.
Joliet, Ill.
Kalamazoo, Mich.
Kenosha, Wis.
Lawrence, Mass.
Lewiston, Me.
Louisville, Ky.
Manchester, N.H.
Michigan City, Ind.
Middletown, Ct.
Minneapolis, Minn.
Mobile, Ala.
Montclair, N.J.
Muncie, Ind.
Muskegon, Mich.
Nashua, N.H.
New Bedford, Mass.
New Orleans, La.
Newport, Ky.
Newport, R.I.
Newton, Mass.
Oklahoma City, Okla.
Oshkosh, Wis.
Passaic, N.J.
Pittsburg, Pa.
Plainfield, N.J.
Portland, Me.
Raleigh, N.C.
Reading, Pa.

Richmond, Ind.
Richmond, Va.
St. Joseph, Mo.
Schenectady, N.Y.
Somerville, Mass.
South Bend, Ind.
South Manchester, Ct.
Springfield, Mass.
Syracuse, N.Y.

Terre Haute, Ind.
Trenton, N.J.
Utica, N.Y.
Waltham, Mass.
Woonsocket, R.I.
Worcester, Mass.

Giving the Tests

The 1,000 words were first made up into 50 lists of 20 words each and these lists were given as dictated spelling tests. Each list of words was first spelled by the children of two consecutive grades in a number of cities. The work was done at the mid-point of the school year and so arranged in each case as to test the spelling attainment of the children who had completed just half the work of each grade. Where words have more than one meaning for the same pronunciation, the meaning desired was indicated by giving a short illustrative sentence.

As a control and check, words were next taken from each of the 50 lists and recombined in new sets of 20 words each and sent out as tests in each of four consecutive grades in the different cities. These two sets of testing were continued until an aggregate of 1,400,000 spellings had been secured from 70,000 children in 84 cities. The results constitute the basis of the present scale.

Problems in Scale Making

To be both valid and convenient, a scale for measuring attainment in spelling should consist of a series of groups of words so arranged that all the words in each group are of equal spelling difficulty, and with the group so arranged that the step in spelling difficulty from any one group to the next higher group will be equal to any other step on the scale from one group to the next higher group.

In the present work, words have been considered as of equal spelling difficulty if they are correctly spelled by an equal proportion of children who have had the same amount of training in spelling, which is to say, by children of the same school grade. It is essential that the words should be of equal difficulty in order to avoid the defect of the ordinary schoolroom test in spelling in which words of greatly varying difficulty are put together in a single 10 or 20 word spelling list, and the pupils' papers marked by taking 10 or 5 points off for each word misspelled. The assumption in such a test is that all the words are equally difficult, whereas this is almost never even approximately true.

The reason why words have been rated as of equal difficulty for given grades in the present study is that it has been found impossible to group them as of equal difficulty for people in general or for school children in general. This is because the easier words are of no difficulty at all for pupils who have had much training, while the same words are of real and varying difficulty for those who have had little training. Similarly, harder words may be of absolute difficulty for children of the lower grades, while they are of varying degrees of difficulty for those of the upper grades. Hence, words can be grouped as of equal difficulty only when we find that they are of equal difficulty for people who have had equal amounts of training; for example, school children of a given grade. Moreover, a valid scale should embrace only words that are normally within the usual writing vocabularies of the children, for otherwise words will be rated as of high degrees of difficulty which are in reality simply unusual. This consideration has been cared for in the present work by confining the entire study to the most commonly used words.

Locating the Equal Steps on the Scale

After the degree of difficulty of each word for pupils of a given grade had been ascertained by finding what per cent of the pupils could spell it correctly, the next proplem was to arrange the words in groups which should be of such progressive degrees of difficulty that all the steps in difficulty from one group to the next, to the next, and so on, should be equal steps. It was necessary to insure that the words in the second group should be as much harder than those in the first, as those in the third were harder than those in the second, and so on for all the successive groups of the scale. The final purpose was to locate these groups at equally spaced steps on a scale from 0 to 100.

The method employed in locating the equal steps on the scale was based on the assumption that spelling ability conforms in general to what is known as the normal distribution.

Spelling Ability and the Normal Distribution

The assumption is based on the well known principle that intellectual abilities are distributed in much the same way among people as are physical traits. Just as there are in a normal population very few dwarfs, many people of about medium height, and very few giants, so there are very few exceedingly poor spellers, many medium ones, and very few truly excellent ones. That this assumption was valid in the present case will be shown later.

The so-called normal curve illustrating such a distribution is reproduced in Diagram 1. The properties of the normal curve have been most accurately determined. Let us suppose that this represents the distribution of spelling ablility among a large number of third grade children.

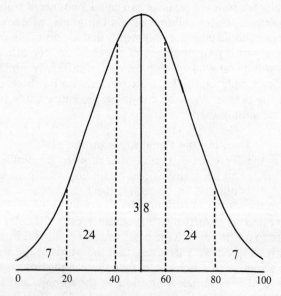

Diagram 1.—Surface of normal distribution with base line five times the sigma distance in length and divided as a scale running from 0 to 100

The area enclosed between the curve and the base line represents all the children ranged according to spelling ability. At the extreme left the curve is very near the base which indicates the small number of very poor spellers. In the middle the curve is distant from the base representing the large proportion of medium spellers. At the right the curve is again very near the base representing the small proportion of excellent spellers. The median line at the 50 per cent point represents the average ability.

The dotted horizontal line from the median to the curve represents the sigma distance and intersects the curve at the point at which it changes from convex to concave. This distance is always a constant function of the curve of normal distribution and in the present study has been chosen as the basis of the measurements along the base line. If we lay out on the base a distance equal to this sigma distance and in such a way that it shall extend equally to the left and right of the 50 per cent point where the median bisects the base, its left end will reach the point marked 40 and its right the one marked 60. If now we lay out the same sigma distance two more times to the left, we shall have the points marked 20 and 0, and by doing the same on the right, we shall have the points marked 80 and 100.

In thus dividing the base into five equal parts, each equal to the sigma distance, and calling the extremes 0 and 100, we are taking liberties with the curve of normal distribution for the base and the curves do not actually meet at these points. In theory the two lines are in asymptote and could be indefinitely extended, always getting nearer together but never touching. In theory about 99.4 per cent of all the cases lie to the right of the point indicated as 0 and some six-tenth of one per cent of them lie to the left. For the purpose of the present study, it has been considered sufficiently accurate to call the point 0 and to assume that all the cases lie to the right. A corresponding assumption is made with respect to the 100 point at the right end of the line.

On the basis of these assumptions, we find that the area of the curve beginning at the left and extending as far as the vertical line at the point 20 is seven per cent of the total. Between this line and the one at point 40 are 24 per cent of the cases, making a total to this point of 31 per cent. From here to point

MEASURING SCALE FOR ABILITY IN SPELLING

A	B	C	D	E	F	G	H	I	J	K	L	M	N	O	P	Q	R	S	T	U	V	W	X	Y	Z	Grade
99	98	96	94	92	88	84	79	73	66	58	50															
100	99	98	96	94	92	88	84	79	73	66	58	50														2nd
	100	99	98	96	94	92	88	84	79	73	66	58	50													
		100	99	98	96	94	92	88	84	79	73	66	58	50												
			100	99	98	96	94	92	88	84	79	73	66	58	50											3rd
				100	99	98	96	94	92	88	84	79	73	66	58	50										
					100	99	98	96	94	92	88	84	79	73	66	58	50									
						100	99	98	96	94	92	88	84	79	73	66	58	50								4th
							100	99	98	96	94	92	88	84	79	73	66	58	50							
								100	99	98	96	94	92	88	84	79	73	66	58	50						
									100	99	98	96	94	92	88	84	79	73	66	58	50					5th
										100	99	98	96	94	92	88	84	79	73	66	58	50				6th
											100	99	98	96	94	92	88	84	79	73	66	58	50			
												100	99	98	96	94	92	88	84	79	73	66	58	50		7th
													100	99	98	96	94	92	88	84	79	73	66	58	50	8th

Diagram 2.—Heading of the scale as finally arranged. This reproduction is one-fourth the length of the actual scale, which is 21 inches long. The words as arranged in List C are printed in the 26 columns from A to Z.

How to use this scale to find a child's spelling level.

STEP 1: Choose one of the alphabetically lettered columns of words on pages 33 thru 39 that you think will let the child show his full range of ability (i.e. a column where he can spell most of the words, but will miss a few). Note the letter name at the top of this column.

STEP 2: Test the child with a list of words randomly selected from the column chosen in step 1, using 20 words if possible. Figure the per cent spelled correctly.

STEP 3: On the above chart, find the column corresponding to the lettered column chosen in step 1. In this column find the per cent which most closely matches the child's score and read his grade level at the end of that row.

60 are 38 per cent, making a total from the beginning of 69 per cent. From this point to point 80 are 24 per cent of the cases, making a total of 93 per cent, and from here to 100 are the remaining seven cases.

Scaling the Words

Now we find that among third grade children in general seven in each 100 fail in the attempt to spell the word *has*, while 93 spell it correctly. Thus if we imagine the normal curve of Diagram 1 as representing 100 typical third grade children ranked according to spelling ability with the worst at the left and the rest in order of ability to the right, we should find that the line at point 20 would fall at such a place that the seven in the 100 who fail on *has* would be to the left of the line while the 93 who can spell it would be on the right. In a similar way the line at 40 would leave on the left the 31 children who fail on *almost* and on its right the 69 who spell it correctly. By this same method all of the words have been located according to their location on a line representing the distance in spelling difficulty from the word so easy that just all can spell it correctly to the one at the other extreme so difficult that none can quite spell it correctly. This is the line from 0 to 100 difficulty and the words have all been located on it according to equal steps of distance.

In order to do this, each of the five divisions shown on the base line of Diagram 1 has been subdivided into five equal parts, making a total of 25 steps for the entire scale from 0 to 100. The average of all the values that might theoretically be contained in each of these 25 steps has thus been determined to the nearest whole number and this value has been assigned to the step. These 25 values are 100, 99, 98, 96, 94, 92, 88, 84, 79, 73, 66, 58, 50, 42, 34, 27, 21, 16, 12, 8, 6, 4, 2, 1, 0. They have been used to identify the 25 steps and they indicate the average per cent of correct spellings found among the children of the grade in question, in their spelling of the words placed on the scale at that step. For example, the nine words, *the*, *in*, *so*, *no*, *now*, *man*, *ten*, *bed*, *top*, are shown on the scale as at step 94 for the second grade. This indicates that the average per cent correct among second grade attempts to spell these words was 94.

Combining the Scales for the Seven Grades

Since the first data returned by the cooperating school systems consisted of figures showing the number of children succeeding and failing in spelling the words in each of two consecutive grades, it was possible to compute the amount of improvement in spelling the same words from grade to grade. It was possible, that is, to find how much better the third grade children spelled the words than the second grade ones, how much better records the fourth grade pupils made than did the third grade ones in spelling the same words, and so on for all the grades.

When these figures, showing average improvement from grade to grade, were reduced to terms of the 25-division spelling scale that has been described on page 30, it was found that the improvement of the third grade over the second averaged about three steps; that of the fourth over the third averaged about three steps; and the improvement of each of the other five grades over its preceding grade averaged about two steps.

These computations of the average shift in spelling ability were then checked up by combining with them the data for the sets of words spelled in four consecutive grades and the results remained nearly unchanged. A further check was then made by computing the shift found from grade to grade by Dr. B. R. Buckingham in his study entitled, "Spelling Ability," published in 1913 by Teachers College, Columbia University. A fourth check was made by comparing with these results those reported by Dr. Buckingham for the use of Dr. J. M. Rice's spelling test. The results of the three investigations all reduced to terms of the 25-step scale of the present study showed average grade shifts as follows:

Grade	Ayres	Buckingham	Rice
2nd to 3rd	2.9	3.2	. .
3rd to 4th	2.9	2.9	. .
4th to 5th	1.9	1.9	2.1
5th to 6th	2.2	2.2	1.8
6th to 7th	1.9	1.6	1.9
7th to 8th	2.0	2.1	2.1
Total	13.8	13.9	

In view of the supporting evidence offered by these several

checks, it was decided to adopt, for combining the several scales into one, shifts in advancing spelling ability from grade to grade as follows: second to third, three steps; third to fourth, three steps; fourth to fifth, two steps; fifth to sixth, two steps; sixth to seventh, two steps; seventh to eighth, two steps.

On this basis the scales for the seven grades were put together, one below the other as illustrated on page 28, so that the third grade scale extends three steps beyond the second grade one; the fourth grade scale is three steps beyond the third grade one; and each of the other scales is located two steps beyond its predecessor.

Testing the Location of the Words

When the headings representing the seven grade scales were thus superimposed on each other with the appropriate shifts from grade to grade, the 1,000 words were entered in the columns below. Their theoretical spelling difficulty in each grade according to the scales was then compared with their difficulties as indicated by the tests in the 84 cities. The results showed that the conformity was so close that if as many as 10 words in one column were considered as a group, the agreement was nearly exact; that among the individual words the very great majority had classroom records in agreement with their scale locations; and that the words spelled in the classrooms by the greatest numbers of children conformed most exactly. These bits of evidence all point in one direction and that is toward the substantiation of the hypothesis that spelling ablilty among homogeneous groups of school children approximately conforms to the normal distribution. If it followed some radically differing type of distribution, the several scales could not fit together as they do.

Final Arrangement of the Scale

In its final arrangement, the scale consists of the seven grade scales so superimposed upon each other as to indicate the approximate shifts from grade to grade and with the 1,000 words entered in 26 columns below. This is shown by the illustration on page 18, which reproduces in miniature the heading of the scale and indicates the columns in which the words are printed in the scale itself. The scale as printed for convenient classroom use will be found in the Appendix with the heading as illustrated on page 18 printed across the top, and the 1000 words entered in the appropriate columns. Preceding the chart, are directions for using the groups of words in measuring children's spelling ability.

In order to facilitate identification and reference, the 26 columns of the scale are designated by the letters from A to Z. The 1,000 words are listed in these columns. In order to complete the record and description as presented in this monograph, these words are published here in Lists B and C beginning on pages 25 and 33 respectively. In List B, the 1,000 words are presented in alphabetic order and beside each is the letter indicating the column in which that word is found on the scale. In List C, the words are presented in columns from A through Z, just as they are published in the scale in its final form.

All the words in each column of the scale are of approximately equal spelling difficulty. The steps in spelling difficulty from each column to the next are approximately equal steps. The numbers at the top of each column on the scale indicate about what per cent of correct spellings of the words in that column may be expected among the children of the different grades. For example, reference to the scale headings as reproduced on page 28 and the words of column H as printed beginning on page 51 will show that if 20 words from this column are given as a spelling test, it may be expected that the average score for an entire second grade spelling them will be about 79 per cent. This will be more clearly understood by referring to the scale as printed on the large sheet for classroom use. The average score for an entire third grade taking the same tests should be about 92 per cent, for a fourth grade about 98 per cent, and for a fifth grade about 100 per cent.

The limits of the groups are as follows: 50 means from 46 through 54 per cent; 58 means from 55 through 62 per cent; 66 means from 63 through 69 per cent; 73 means from 70 through 76 per cent; 79 means from 77 through 81 per cent; 84 means from 82 through 86 per cent; 88 means from 87 through 90 per cent; 92 means from 91 through 93 per cent; 94 means 94 and 95 per cent; 96 means 96 and 97 per cent; while 98, 99 and 100 per cent are separate groups.

By means of these groupings, a child's spelling ability may

be located in terms of grades. Thus, if a child were given a 20 word spelling test from the words of column O and spelled 15 words, or 75 per cent of them, correctly, it would be proper to say that he showed fourth grade spelling ability. If he spelled correctly 17 words, or 85 per cent, he would show fifth grade ability, and so on.

All of the scales have been arbitrarily cut off at 50 per cent, partly because it is doubtful whether any useful teaching purpose is served by testing children on words of which they cannot spell more than 50 per cent correctly, and partly because children of the lower grades attempting to spell difficult words frequently fail, not because of the inherent difficulty of the spelling, but because the word form is not yet definitely a part of the children's regular vocabulary. Thus the record in spelling these words becomes unreliable and it was considered wisest to omit from the scale the numbers showing the scores which children spelling such words would make.

Length of Words and Spelling Difficulty

A mere inspection of the scale shows that practically all of the easier words in the first columns are monosyllables. In the middle of the scale are many words of medium difficulty and medium length. At the right hand are found words of greater difficulty and greater length. Thus it is clear that there is a considerable positive correlation between length and difficulty. If we consider the respective difficulties of the words in the 26 columns as being represented by consecutive numbers running from 1 to 26 and compute the correlation between these difficulties and the lengths of the words in these columns, we get a Pearson coefficient of correlation of .734. The close relationship between the length of the words and their difficulty is probably to be accounted for in part by the fact that mere length tends to increase spelling difficulty and in addition, the longer the word is, the more opportunities it presents for difficult combinations of letters and difficulties arising through inaccurate pronunciation. The correlation between the spelling difficulties and the lengths of the words, computed by the Spearman method, gives a coefficient of .882, while the percentage of unlike signed pairs gives a coefficient of .767 and Galton's graphic method one of .78.

Use and Limitations

The scale that has been produced by this study should be found useful in three ways. In the first place, it consists of a list of 1,000 words which probably constitute a most valuable foundation spelling vocabulary.

In the second place, these words are presented in the final scale in groups of approximately equal spelling difficulty. These groups, which are also printed as List C of the present publication, furnish more reliable material for spelling tests than has heretofore been available. This is because the words of each list are of nearly equal difficulty and hence in using them in spelling tests all of the units of the test are of nearly equal value.

In the third place, the scale is so arranged as to indicate about what percentage of children in the several grades in cities throughout the country succeed in spelling the words correctly. By means of these standards children of the different grades in any locality may be tested as to their spelling attainment and the results compared with those which are found in the corresponding grades in city systems in general. When such tests are made of the spelling attainment of large numbers of children in the different grades in any one locality, the results may be compared with considerable reliability with those here presented for the 84 cities which cooperated in the present study. With less reliability the attainment of a smaller number of grades or of one grade may be tested. With still less reliability the attainment of a single child may be compared with these average results.

In all such testing it must be remembered that the present scale or any scale for measuring spelling attainment will become increasingly and rapidly less reliable for measuring purposes as the children become more accustomed to spelling these particular words. In proportion as these lists are used for the purposes of classroom drill, the scale will become untrustworthy as a measuring instrument. Probably the scale will have served its greatest usefulness in any locality when the school children have mastered these 1,000 words so thoroughly that the scale has become quite useless as a measuring instrument.

LIST B. The thousand words arranged in alphabetic order. The letters indicate the columns in which the words are located in the final scale.

a	C	an	E	baby	H
able	L	and	B	back	I
aboard	O	annual	X	bad	E
about	H	another	L	ball	H
above	L	answer	P	band	J
absence	T	any	K	be	F
accept	T	anything	L	bear	K
accident	T	anyway	M	beautiful	P
according	R	appear	O	became	K
account	M	application	U	because	L
across	K	appoint	Q	become	K
act	N	appreciate	W	bed	D
action	Q	April	N	been	N
add	I	are	G	before	L
addition	Q	argument	T	beg	P
address	O	army	M	began	L
adopt	R	around	K	begin	M
affair	S	arrange	Q	beginning	U
afraid	O	arrangement	V	begun	M
after	I	arrest	Q	behind	K
afternoon	K	arrive	S	believe	S
again	M	article	R	belong	H
against	R	as	H	beside	M
age	J	ask	H	best	I
ago	E	assist	S	better	K
agreement	U	associate	T	between	O
air	J	association	V	big	G
alike	I	assure	U	bill	J
all	F	at	B	black	L
allege	Z	athletic	W	block	I
allow	Q	attempt	Q	blow	I
almost	M	attend	O	blue	J
alone	L	attention	R	board	O
along	J	August	O	boat	J
already	R	aunt	N	body	L
also	M	auto	P	book	F
although	Q	automobile	T	born	M
always	N	avenue	R	both	M
am	E	await	Q	bought	M
among	N	away	I	box	H
amount	P	awful	P	boy	F

bridge	N	circular	T	cover	J
bring	H	circumstance	U	crowd	Q
broke	N	cities	P	cut	I
brother	K	citizen	U	dark	J
brought	M	city	K	dash	L
build	M	claim	Q	date	L
built	N	class	K	daughter	P
burn	K	clean	K	day	H
business	T	clear	K	dead	L
busy	R	clerk	P	deal	M
but	F	close	L	dear	I
buy	L	clothing	L	death	N
by	G	club	K	debate	Q
call	H	cold	G	December	N
came	I	collect	M	decide	T
camp	K	colonies	U	decision	Y
can	C	combination	R	declare	Q
cannot	J	come	G	deep	J
capture	N	comfort	O	degree	P
car	J	coming	K	delay	K
card	J	command	Q	department	P
care	K	committee	X	desire	P
career	V	common	R	destroy	P
carried	P	company	O	develop	U
carry	N	complaint	P	diamond	R
case	M	complete	R	did	F
cast	J	concern	T	died	M
catch	L	condition	S	difference	S
cause	N	conference	T	different	R
celebration	T	connection	Q	difficulty	U
cent	K	consider	R	direct	O
center	N	consideration	U	direction	Q
century	S	contain	O	director	R
certain	S	contract	M	disappoint	X
chain	N	convenient	X	discussion	V
change	M	convention	R	distinguish	U
character	W	convict	Q	distribute	R
charge	M	copy	N	district	O
check	N	cordially	W	divide	U
chief	O	cost	K	do	A
child	G	could	K	doctor	N
children	M	country	L	does	P
Christmas	R	course	S	dollar	N
church	L	court	N	done	L

don't	O	estimate	T	find	I
door	H	even	K	fine	J
doubt	S	evening	N	finish	K
down	J	event	M	fire	J
dozen	N	ever	L	firm	Q
dress	M	every	J	first	K
drill	M	everything	O	five	H
driven	M	evidence	V	fix	M
drown	R	examination	S	flight	P
due	Q	except	N	flower	L
during	O	expect	N	folks	T
duty	O	expense	U	follow	M
each	I	experience	V	foot	I
earliest	U	express	L	for	H
early	L	extra	M	foreign	U
east	J	extreme	W	forenoon	R
easy	K	eye	K	forget	J
eat	H	face	I	form	I
education	R	fact	O	fortune	P
effect	R	factory	Q	forty	O
effort	Q	fail	K	forward	Q
eight	O	fair	N	found	J
either	Q	fall	I	four	L
elaborate	U	family	P	fourth	O
elect	O	famous	Q	free	I
election	P	far	I	Friday	K
else	N	farther	O	friend	O
emergency	W	father	L	from	J
empire	P	favor	P	front	N
employ	Q	feature	R	full	K
enclose	Q	February	W	further	S
end	I	feel	N	game	J
engage	Q	feet	I	gave	I
engine	P	fell	L	general	R
enjoy	P	felt	K	gentleman	Q
enough	O	few	M	get	H
enter	M	field	Q	getting	O
entertain	R	fifth	N	girl	J
entire	Q	fight	L	give	I
entitle	T	figure	O	glad	J
entrance	P	file	M	glass	K
escape	P	fill	J	go	B
especially	X	final	Q	God	N
estate	Q	finally	U	goes	M

gold	J	how	H	keep	K
gone	L	however	L	kill	G
good	E	human	P	kind	J
got	I	hurt	K	knew	O
government	S	husband	P	know	L
grand	J	I	H	known	P
grant	L	ice	G	lady	K
great	M	if	H	lake	I
ground	L	illustrate	R	land	G
guess	T	immediate	X	large	J
guest	P	importance	P	last	E
had	G	important	Q	late	G
half	L	impossible	T	law	H
hand	G	imprison	Q	lay	H
happen	M	improvement	S	lead	L
happy	J	in	D	learn	N
hard	J	include	Q	least	N
has	H	income	M	leave	L
hat	G	increase	R	led	H
have	G	indeed	L	ledge	Q
he	E	inform	M	left	J
head	K	information	Q	length	P
hear	N	injure	R	less	M
heard	N	inside	J	lesson	L
heart	M	inspect	N	let	G
height	V	instead	O	letter	I
held	L	intend	O	liberty	O
help	J	interest	R	life	J
her	H	into	F	light	K
here	J	investigate	S	like	F
herself	L	invitation	T	line	J
high	L	is	C	list	L
him	F	issue	U	little	E
himself	N	it	C	live	G
his	H	its	I	local	S
history	N	itself	N	long	H
hold	M	jail	O	look	F
home	H	January	N	lose	R
honor	R	judge	O	loss	P
hope	J	judgment	Z	lost	J
horse	K	July	K	lot	H
hot	G	June	L	love	H
hour	K	just	H	low	H
house	H	justice	Q	machine	R

madam	O	much	H	omit	M
made	J	must	G	on	B
mail	K	my	E	once	L
majority	U	name	J	one	H
make	G	national	T	only	K
man	D	navy	O	open	K
manner	R	near	J	opinion	S
many	L	nearly	P	or	I
March	L	necessary	U	order	L
marriage	S	need	N	organization	W
material	U	neighbor	R	organize	T
matter	N	neither	S	other	H
May	J	never	J	ought	T
may	F	new	I	our	J
maybe	K	news	L	out	F
mayor	P	newspaper	P	outside	J
me	A	next	L	over	G
mean	N	nice	I	own	L
meant	U	night	K	page	I
measure	Q	nine	I	paid	M
meet	L	no	D	pair	N
member	M	none	O	paper	I
men	H	noon	J	part	J
mention	S	nor	N	particular	S
mere	U	north	I	party	K
might	M	not	E	pass	K
mile	K	nothing	L	past	M
mind	L	November	N	pay	J
mine	J	now	D	people	L
minute	T	number	N	perfect	O
Miss	M	object	R	perhaps	Q
miss	I	objection	O	period	Q
Monday	I	oblige	P	person	N
money	M	obtain	P	personal	O
month	M	occupy	U	picture	M
more	J	o'clock	P	piece	S
morning	L	October	N	place	J
most	J	of	F	plan	N
mother	G	off	M	plant	I
motion	S	offer	N	play	G
mountain	M	office	M	pleasant	S
move	K	official	T	please	M
Mr.	I	often	S	pleasure	O
Mrs.	P	old	E	point	L

police	O	railroad	M	road	L
political	T	rain	K	room	J
poor	K	raise	O	round	K
popular	R	ran	H	royal	O
population	O	rapid	P	rule	N
position	Q	rate	O	run	C
possible	S	rather	O	running	Q
post	J	reach	K	said	J
pound	K	read	J	sail	P
power	L	ready	M	salary	R
practical	W	real	M	same	J
prefer	R	really	T	Saturday	Q
preliminary	X	reason	N	saw	J
prepare	R	receipt	X	say	G
present	Q	receive	U	says	M
president	Q	recent	T	scene	U
press	N	recommend	Z	school	G
pretty	M	recover	M	sea	G
price	K	red	E	search	R
primary	Q	refer	T	second	O
principal	V	reference	V	secretary	V
principle	Y	refuse	O	section	Q
print	J	regard	P	secure	R
prison	P	region	Q	see	C
private	Q	relative	Q	seem	K
probably	U	relief	U	seen	K
proceed	W	remain	O	select	Q
progress	Q	remember	Q	senate	U
promise	R	repair	P	send	H
prompt	Q	reply	P	sent	K
proper	O	report	J	separate	W
property	Q	represent	Q	September	O
prove	N	request	O	serious	S
provide	M	respectfully	U	serve	Q
provision	R	responsible	U	service	R
public	O	rest	J	session	V
publication	R	restrain	O	set	K
publish	Q	result	Q	seven	J
purpose	R	retire	O	several	P
push	L	return	M	shall	L
put	I	ride	I	she	C
question	N	right	L	shed	O
quite	O	ring	G	ship	J
race	J	river	I	short	K

should	K	stood	M	there	N
show	I	stop	L	therefore	S
shut	K	stopped	S	these	K
sick	I	story	K	they	K
side	J	street	G	thing	I
sight	M	struck	O	think	J
since	P	study	N	third	L
sincerely	W	subject	N	this	F
sir	K	success	R	those	M
sister	J	such	L	though	P
sit	H	sudden	O	thought	N
six	F	suffer	N	three	G
size	N	suggest	U	through	O
slide	O	suit	L	throw	O
small	L	summer	L	Thursday	O
so	D	summon	T	thus	N
soap	L	Sunday	I	ticket	M
soft	H	supply	S	time	F
sold	I	support	P	tire	N
some	H	suppose	Q	to	H
something	N	sure	N	today	F
sometimes	Q	surprise	Q	together	R
son	J	system	S	told	I
song	I	table	L	tomorrow	R
soon	I	take	I	tonight	K
sorry	N	talk	L	too	S
south	J	tax	N	took	M
speak	M	teach	M	top	D
special	Q	teacher	N	total	S
spell	K	tell	H	toward	R
spend	P	ten	D	town	J
spent	I	tenth	K	track	L
spring	I	term	Q	train	J
stamp	K	terrible	Q	travel	P
stand	H	testimony	V	treasure	R
start	K	than	I	tree	I
state	K	thank	I	trip	L
statement	Q	that	H	trouble	P
station	O	the	D	true	M
stay	J	theater	S	truly	O
steamer	M	their	Q	trust	M
still	J	them	H	try	K
stole	M	themselves	Q	Tuesday	O
stone	I	then	H	turn	L

two	K	watch	L	wire	M
unable	M	water	K	wish	L
uncle	O	way	H	with	J
under	J	we	E	within	L
understand	M	wear	R	without	K
unfortunate	U	weather	O	witness	S
unless	L	Wednesday	T	woman	N
until	O	week	K	women	Q
up	E	weigh	R	wonder	N
upon	K	well	H	wonderful	Q
us	E	went	I	word	J
use	N	were	L	work	J
usual	P	west	I	world	L
vacation	P	what	I	worth	O
various	T	when	J	would	K
very	I	where	K	wreck	R
vessel	R	whether	U	write	N
victim	T	which	P	written	Q
view	P	while	M	wrote	N
visit	P	white	I	yard	H
visitor	R	who	M	year	H
volume	T	whole	O	yes	H
vote	N	whom	Q	yesterday	N
wait	P	whose	Q	yet	I
walk	L	why	J	you	E
want	J	wife	K	young	N
war	L	will	E	your	F
warm	L	wind	J		
was	H	winter	I		

LIST C. The thousand words arranged in the order in which they appear in the final scale. The twenty-six groups given here under the letters from A to Z are printed under the same letters on the scale.

A		come	get
me	us	hand	home
do	am	ring	much
	good	live	call
	little	kill	long
B	ago	late	love
and	old	let	then
go	bad	big	house
at	red	mother	year
on		three	to
	F	land	I
C	of	cold	as
a	be	hot	send
it	but	hat	one
is	this	child	has
she	all	ice	some
can	your	play	if
see	out	sea	how
run	time		her
	may		them
D	into	**H**	other
the	him	day	baby
in	today	eat	well
so	look	sit	about
no	did	lot	men
now	like	box	for
man	six	belong	ran
ten	boy	door	was
bed	book	yes	that
top		low	his
	G	soft	led
E	by	stand	lay
he	have	yard	
you	are	bring	
will	had	tell	**I**
we	over	five	nine
an	must	ball	face
my	make	law	miss
up	school	ask	ride
last	street	just	tree
not	say	way	sick

got	very	age	fill
north	or	gold	along
while	thank	read	lost
spent	dear	fine	name
foot	west	cannot	room
blow	sold	May	hope
block	told	line	same
spring	best	left	glad
river	form	ship	with
plant	far	train	mine
cut	gave	saw	
song	alike	pay	**K**
winter	add	large	became
stone		near	brother
free	**J**	down	rain
lake	seven	why	keep
page	forget	bill	start
nice	happy	want	mail
end	noon	girl	eye
fall	think	part	glass
feet	sister	still	party
went	cast	place	upon
back	card	report	two
away	south	never	they
paper	deep	found	would
put	inside	side	any
each	blue	kind	could
soon	post	life	should
came	town	here	city
Sunday	stay	car	only
show	grand	word	where
Monday	outside	every	week
yet	dark	under	first
find	band	most	sent
give	game	made	mile
new	boat	said	seem
letter	rest	work	even
take	east	our	without
Mr.	son	more	afternoon
after	help	when	Friday
thing	hard	from	hour
what	race	wind	wife
than	cover	print	state
its	fire	air	July

head	coming	road	done
story	cent	March	body
open	night	next	
short	pass	indeed	**M**
lady	shut	four	trust
reach	easy	herself	extra
better		power	dress
water	**L**	wish	beside
round	catch	because	teach
cost	black	world	happen
price	warm	country	begun
become	unless	meet	collect
class	clothing	another	file
horse	began	trip	provide
care	able	list	sight
try	gone	people	stood
move	suit	ever	fix
delay	track	held	born
pound	watch	church	goes
behind	dash	once	hold
around	fell	own	drill
burn	fight	before	army
camp	buy	know	pretty
bear	stop	were	stole
clear	walk	dead	income
clean	grant	leave	bought
spell	soap	early	paid
poor	news	close	enter
finish	small	flower	railroad
hurt	war	nothing	unable
maybe	summer	ground	ticket
across	above	lead	account
tonight	express	such	driven
tenth	turn	many	real
sir	lesson	morning	recover
these	half	however	mountain
club	father	mind	steamer
seen	anything	shall	speak
felt	table	alone	past
full	high	order	might
fail	talk	third	begin
set	June	push	contract
stamp	right	point	deal
light	date	within	almost

brought
less
event
off
true
took
again
inform
both
heart
month
children
build
understand
follow
charge
says
member
case
while
also
return
those
office
great
Miss
who
died
change
wire
few
please
picture
money
ready
omit
anyway

N
except
aunt
capture
wrote
else

bridge
offer
suffer
built
center
front
rule
carry
chain
death
learn
wonder
tire
pair
check
prove
heard
inspect
itself
always
something
write
expect
need
thus
woman
young
fair
dollar
evening
plan
broke
feel
sure
least
sorry
press
God
teacher
November
subject
April
history
cause

study
himself
matter
use
thought
person
nor
January
mean
vote
court
copy
act
been
yesterday
among
question
doctor
hear
size
December
dozen
there
tax
number
October
reason
fifth

O
eight
afraid
uncle
rather
comfort
elect
aboard
jail
shed
retire
refuse
district
restrain
royal

objection
pleasure
navy
fourth
population
proper
judge
weather
worth
contain
figure
sudden
forty
instead
throw
personal
everything
rate
chief
perfect
second
slide
farther
duty
intend
company
quite
none
knew
remain
direct
appear
liberty
enough
fact
board
September
station
attend
between
public
friend
during
through
police

until	family	firm	justice
madam	favor	region	gentleman
truly	Mrs.	convict	enclose
whole	husband	private	await
address	amount	command	suppose
request	human	debate	wonderful
raise	view	crowd	direction
August	election	factory	forward
Tuesday	clerk	publish	although
struck	though	represent	prompt
getting	o'clock	term	attempt
don't	support	section	whose
Thursday	does	relative	statement
	regard	progress	perhaps
P	escape	entire	their
spend	since	president	imprison
enjoy	which	measure	written
awful	length	famous	arrange
usual	destroy	serve	
complaint	newspaper	estate	**R**
auto	daughter	remember	forenoon
vacation	answer	either	lose
beautiful	reply	effort	combination
flight	oblige	important	avenue
travel	sail	due	neighbor
rapid	cities	include	weigh
repair	known	running	wear
trouble	several	allow	entertain
entrance	desire	position	salary
importance	nearly	field	visitor
carried		ledge	publication
lose	**Q**	claim	machine
fortune	sometimes	primary	toward
empire	declare	result	success
mayor	engage	Saturday	drown
wait	final	appoint	adopt
beg	terrible	information	secure
degree	surprise	whom	honor
prison	period	arrest	promise
engine	addition	themselves	wreck
visit	employ	special	prepare
guest	property	women	vessel
department	select	present	busy
obtain	connection	action	prefer

illustrate	assist	decide	agreement
different	difference	entitle	unfortunate
object	examination	political	majority
provision	particular	national	elaborate
according	affair	recent	citizen
already	course	business	necessary
attention	neither	refer	divide
education	local	minute	
director	marriage	ought	**V**
purpose	further	absence	principal
common	serious	conference	testimony
diamond	doubt	Wednesday	discussion
together	condition	really	arrangement
convention	government	celebration	reference
increase	opinion	folks	evidence
manner	believe		experience
feature	system	**U**	session
article	possible	meant	secretary
service	piece	earliest	association
injure	certain	whether	career
effect	witness	distinguish	height
distribute	investigate	consideration	
general	therefore	colonies	**W**
tomorrow	too	assure	organization
consider	pleasant	relief	emergency
against		occupy	appreciate
complete		probably	sincerely
search	**T**	foreign	athletic
treasure	guess	expense	extreme
popular	circular	responsible	practical
Christmas	argument	beginning	proceed
interest	volume	application	cordially
	organize	difficulty	character
	summon	scene	separate
S	official	finally	February
often	victim	develop	
stopped	estimate	circumstance	**X**
motion	accident	issue	immediate
theater	invitation	material	convenient
improvement	accept	suggest	receipt
century	impossible	mere	preliminary
total	concern	senate	disappoint
mention	associate	receive	especially
arrive	automobile	respectfully	annual
supply	various		

APPENDIX

Full Spelling Scale

In this appendix, the word lists and the heading of the scale are combined for greater ease of use. Across the top of the following pages, is the heading of the scale which is found on page 18 of the main text. Notice the grade levels in the first column of the heading. These are repeated on each left-hand page for your convenience.

Beneath each column of the heading is its own word list. Thus you have together on one page the test list you choose to use and the scores which go with it.

Follow these three simple steps for measuring with this scale.

1. Choose one of the alphabetically lettered columns of words that you think will let the child show his full range of ability (i.e. a column where the child can spell most of the words, but will miss a few).

2. Test the child with a list of words randomly selected from the column chosen in step 1, using 20 words if possible. Figure the per cent spelled correctly.

3. From the heading of the column, find the per cent which most closely matches the child's score, and read his grade level at the left end of that row.

After seeing their scores on this scale, children are often motivated to improve their spelling. Then the words in the scale can be put to a second use—spelling study. Knowledge of these words takes spellers a long way toward their goal, since these words make up such a large percentage of everyday writing.

Those who believe in a phonics approach to spelling (rather than a common-word approach) may still use these words, but teach them by a phonics method. The words a child misses are good clues to the phonics he needs to learn. Thus, diagnosing is still another use of the scale.

So there are three major ways you may use this scale: 1) measure, 2) diagnose, 3) teach.

GRADE LEVEL	A	B	C	D	E
2	99	98	96	94	92
3			100	99	98
4					
5					
6					
7					
8					
	me do	and go at on	a it is she can see run	the in so no now man ten bed top	he you will we an my up last not us am good little ago old bad red

F	G	H	I
88	84	79	73
96	94	92	88
100	99	98	96
		100	99

F	G	H		I	
of	by	day	then	nine	each
be	have	eat	house	face	soon
but	are	sit	year	miss	came
this	had	lot	to	ride	Sunday
all	over	box	I	tree	show
your	must	belong	as	sick	Monday
out	make	door	send	got	yet
time	school	yes	one	north	find
may	street	low	has	white	give
into	say	soft	some	spent	new
him	come	stand	if	foot	letter
today	hand	yard	how	blow	take
look	ring	bring	her	block	Mr.
did	live	tell	them	spring	after
like	kill	five	other	river	thing
six	late	ball	baby	plant	what
boy	let	law	well	cut	than
book	big	ask	about	song	its
	mother	just	men	winter	very
	three	way	for	stone	or
	land	get	ran	free	thank
	cold	home	was	lake	dear
	hot	much	that	page	west
	hat	call	his	nice	sold
	child	long	led	end	told
	ice	love	lay	fall	best
	play			feet	form
	sea			went	far
				back	gave
				away	alike
				paper	add
				put	

GRADE LEVEL	J	K
2	66	58
3	84	79
4	94	92
5	98	96
6	100	99
7		
8		

J

seven	line	wind
forget	left	print
happy	ship	air
noon	train	fill
think	saw	along
sister	pay	lost
cast	large	name
card	near	room
south	down	hope
deep	why	same
inside	bill	glad
blue	want	with
post	girl	mine
town	part	
stay	still	
grand	place	
outside	report	
dark	never	
band	found	
game	side	
boat	kind	
rest	life	
east	here	
son	car	
help	word	
hard	every	
race	under	
cover	most	
fire	made	
age	said	
gold	work	
read	our	
fine	more	
cannot	when	
May	from	

K

became	short	felt
brother	lady	full
rain	reach	fail
keep	better	set
start	water	stamp
mail	round	light
eye	cost	coming
glass	price	cent
party	become	night
upon	class	pass
two	horse	shut
they	care	easy
would	try	
any	move	
could	delay	
should	pound	
city	behind	
only	around	
where	burn	
week	camp	
first	bear	
sent	clear	
mile	clean	
seem	spell	
even	poor	
without	finish	
afternoon	hurt	
Friday	maybe	
hour	across	
wife	tonight	
state	tenth	
July	sir	
head	these	
story	club	
open	seen	

L	M
50	
73	66
88	84
94	92
98	96
100	99

catch	date	morning	trust	might	few
black	road	however	extra	begin	please
warm	March	mind	dress	contract	picture
unless	next	shall	beside	deal	money
clothing	indeed	alone	teach	almost	ready
began	four	order	happen	brought	omit
able	herself	third	begun	less	anyway
gone	power	push	collect	event	
suit	wish	point	file	off	
track	because	within	provide	true	
watch	world	done	sight	took	
dash	country	body	stood	again	
fell	meet		fix	inform	
fight	another		born	both	
buy	trip		goes	heart	
stop	list		hold	month	
walk	people		drill	children	
grant	ever		army	build	
soap	held		pretty	understand	
news	church		stole	follow	
small	once		income	charge	
war	own		bought	says	
summer	before		paid	member	
above	know		enter	case	
express	were		railroad	while	
turn	dead		unable	also	
lesson	leave		ticket	return	
half	early		account	those	
father	close		driven	office	
anything	flower		real	great	
table	nothing		recover	Miss	
high	ground		mountain	who	
talk	lead		steamer	died	
June	such		speak	change	
right	many		past	wire	

GRADE LEVEL	N	O
2		
3	**58**	**50**
4	**79**	**73**
5	**88**	**84**
6	**94**	**92**
7	**98**	**96**
8	**100**	**99**

N			O	
except	broke	tax	eight	farther
aunt	feel	number	afraid	duty
capture	sure	October	uncle	intend
wrote	least	reason	rather	company
else	sorry	fifth	comfort	quite
bridge	press		elect	none
offer	God		aboard	knew
suffer	teacher		jail	remain
built	November		shed	direct
center	subject		retire	appear
front	April		refuse	liberty
rule	history		district	enough
carry	cause		restrain	fact
chain	study		royal	board
death	himself		objection	September
learn	matter		pleasure	station
wonder	use		navy	attend
tire	thought		fourth	between
pair	person		population	public
check	nor		proper	friend
prove	January		judge	during
heard	mean		weather	through
inspect	vote		worth	police
itself	court		contain	until
always	copy		figure	madam
something	act		sudden	truly
write	been		forty	whole
expect	yesterday		instead	address
need	among		throw	request
thus	question		personal	raise
woman	doctor		everything	August
young	hear		rate	Tuesday
fair	size		chief	struck
dollar	December		perfect	getting
evening	dozen		second	don't
plan	there		slide	Thursday

P		Q		
66		58		
79		73		
88		84		
94		92		
98		96		

P		Q		
spend	view	sometimes	due	imprison
enjoy	election	declare	include	written
awful	clerk	engage	running	arrange
usual	though	final	allow	factory
complaint	o'clock	terrible	position	
auto	support	surprise	field	
vacation	does	period	ledge	
beautiful	regard	addition	claim	
flight	escape	employ	primary	
travel	since	property	result	
rapid	which	select	Saturday	
repair	length	connection	appoint	
trouble	destroy	firm	information	
entrance	newspaper	region	whom	
importance	daughter	convict	arrest	
carried	answer	private	themselves	
loss	reply	command	special	
fortune	oblige	debate	women	
empire	sail	crowd	present	
mayor	cities	publish	action	
wait	known	represent	justice	
beg	several	term	gentleman	
degree	desire	section	enclose	
prison	nearly	relative	await	
engine		progress	suppose	
visit		entire	wonderful	
guest		president	direction	
department		measure	forward	
obtain		famous	although	
family		serve	prompt	
favor		estate	attempt	
Mrs.		remember	whose	
husband		either	statement	
amount		effort	perhaps	
human		important	their	

GRADE LEVEL	R	S	T
2			
3			
4	50		
5	66	58	50
6	79	73	66
7	88	84	79
8	94	92	88

R		S	T
forenoon	diamond	often	guess
lose	together	stopped	circular
combination	convention	motion	argument
avenue	increase	theater	volume
neighbor	manner	improvement	organize
weigh	feature	century	summon
wear	article	total	official
entertain	service	mention	victim
salary	injure	arrive	estimate
visitor	effect	supply	accident
publication	distribute	assist	invitation
machine	general	difference	accept
toward	tomorrow	examination	impossible
success	consider	particular	concern
drown	against	affair	associate
adopt	complete	course	automobile
secure	search	neither	various
honor	treasure	local	decide
promise	popular	marriage	entitle
wreck	Christmas	further	political
prepare	interest	serious	national
vessel		doubt	recent
busy		condition	business
prefer		government	refer
illustrate		opinion	minute
different		believe	ought
object		system	absence
provision		possible	conference
according		piece	Wednesday
already		certain	really
attention		witness	celebration
education		investigate	folks
director		therefore	
purpose		too	
common		pleasant	

U	V	W
58	50	
73	66	58
84	79	73

U	V	W
meant	principal	organization
earliest	testimony	emergency
whether	discussion	appreciate
distinguish	arrangement	sincerely
consideration	reference	athletic
colonies	evidence	extreme
assure	experience	practical
relief	session	proceed
occupy	secretary	cordially
probably	association	character
foreign	career	separate
expense	height	February
responsible		
beginning		
application		
difficulty		
scene		
finally		
develop		
circumstance		
issue		
material		
suggest		
mere		
senate		
receive		
respectfully		
agreement		
unfortunate		
majority		
elaborate		
citizen		
necessary		
divide		

GRADE LEVEL	X	Y	Z
2			
3			
4			
5			
6			
7	50		
8	66	58	50
	immediate convenient receipt preliminary disappoint especially annual committee	decision principle	judgment recommend allege

NOTES

NOTES

More Phonics and Spelling Help

THE ABC'S AND ALL THEIR TRICKS by Margaret M. Bishop. THE phonics book for teachers. A monumental work which is only possible since the onset of computerized studies of English words. Comprehensive information is given here for every spelling of every sound. For each spelling you find rules which govern it, exceptions to the rules, sample words to use for teaching the sound or spelling, etymological information, and an interesting little statistic of frequency. When you look up *QU* as in queen, for instance, you find 220 words have this blend. The following page has *QU* as in bouquet, and you find only 40 words contain that sound/spelling. So this tells you which is most useful for children to know. Several appendices give information on such matters as suffixes, spelling rules, and remedial teaching. With this book in your classroom, you will never have to say "I don't know" to a question of phonics.

PHONICS MADE PLAIN by Michael S. Brunner. This set consists of flashcards and a wall chart for classroom use. On one side of each card is a phonogram to display to your class and on the reverse side is teaching information for you. The correlated wall chart does indeed make phonics plain, as you see everything organized into ten manageable groups. You CAN teach them. Your children CAN learn. Instructions included.

MRS. SILVER'S PHONICS WORKBOOK 1 by Claudine Silver. This course, the first in a series, is for beginners who need to learn consonant sounds and short vowel sounds. In the McGuffey system, it is used before the Primers. The teacher's edition contains complete instructions for using the workbook and for enriching the lessons with additional activities. With phonics, children can build a wide knowledge of words and ideas. To help with this, Mrs. Silver gives words for science, music, Bible, and other curriculum areas, and ideas for correlating them with each phonics lesson.

RICE CHRISTIAN READER AND SPELLER by Carolyn Rose and Karma Hudson. This unique teaching aid follows in the tradition of Webster's famous *Blue Back Speller*, providing word lists organized according to spelling rules. As children drill on these lists, they learn the power of letters. Useful at all levels from alphabet learning up to difficult four-syllable words.

PHONICS IN SONG by Leon V. Metcalf. Delightful, catchy melodies teach each letter of the alphabet and the most important digraphs— *ch*, *sh*, *th*, and *wh*. A sing-along tape is also available.

These books are available from:
Mott Media
Milford, Michigan 48042